RECIPES OF
West Bengal

MINAKSHI GANGULI

INDIA • SINGAPORE • MALAYSIA

ISBN 979-8-89363-998-8

Preface

My children asked me to consolidate recipes of Bengali home food that they grow up with and my own tried and tested recipes. The recipes have been used by my family for generations, and then by me during the growing years of my children. The recipes are for a captive group of interested cooks who are willing to try them out.

The recipes are very quick and easy to cook with minimum effort and simple ingredients. This is not an effort to compete with professional cooks and their cookbooks. The taste of the food is very mild as in regular food of Bengal and not to be compared with the Mughlai, Chettinad, Malabar, Bukhara, cuisines to name a few.

The state of Bengal falls on the northeastern end of India. Before the partition of India both East Bengal and West Bengal were jointly called Bengal. When India was divided into India and Pakistan by the British during independence, the northern part of Bengal was named East Bengal and governed by Pakistan and the southern part was called West Bengal, which was governed by India.

In 1963, with the aide of Indian military presence, India fought with Pakistan. East Bengal became a new country called Bangladesh. The food habits and taste of the east Bengalis (Bangladesh) are quite different and distinguishable from the cuisine of West Bengal as they were named. A simple but important difference is the use of sugar in West Bengal cooking. Bangladeshis do not use sweeteners, except in dessert and chutneys. My knowledge of Bengali cooking is restricted to the West Bengal style.

Kolkata, the capital of West Bengal has some dishes of its own, influenced by the British. The Anglo-Indian version of food which the locals cooked for the British improvised recipes to suit the Indian climate. From this experiment, evolved the ever-popular Mulligatawny soup and soup in general, which the average Bengalis did not have.

Although, most of our population know English, there is a mixture of the language for which all the recipes have a Bengali name with an English, translated name in parathees so that the Bengali speaking cook is familiar and comfortable, and the others can also understand. There are some words which are common in Bengali and English and Hindi so everyone can follow directions.

Bengali's love their food. Their day-to-day lunches and dinners consist of at least 3 or 4 dishes with one fish preparation. They are rice eaters and fish with rice is a common feature in most homes.

Traditionally Bengali food is served in large plates otherwise called thala with small bowls on the side filled with lentils, vegetables, fish, meat etc. Rice is served on the center of the plate with a pinch of salt and a wedge of lemon placed for individual taste. Each item is eaten separately with the rice, the vegetables, lentils are eaten first, followed by fish/ meat chutney, and end with sweet yoghurt and the dessert of the day.

Happy Cooking!

Contents

Rice Dishes

Bhat (Cooked Rice)

🥣 Ingredients

- 2 teacups rice
- 4 teacups water

The quality of rice is very important in Kolkata. The poor or even the middle class stick to a traditional brand of rice that they prefer. The rich normally stick to fragrant long-grained rice which is white in color, quick to cook and expensive. The parboiled rice or brown rice is light brown in color, may be expensive or cheaper and more nutritious and takes longer to cook.

The long-grained rice takes a shorter time to cook. Wash the rice several times till the water runs clear and set it to boil with 4 cups water. Once the water starts boiling, turn down the heat and cover till the grains are done (about 6 to 8 min). Once it is done, pour more boiled water and strain the water till all the water is drained, as this will take out the excess starch.

The parboiled rice takes at least ½ hour to cook through in the same manner, so it is helpful to use a pressure cooker where it takes a minute after the whistle blows. Outside Bengal, rice is also cooked either in a rice cooker in 1:2 ratio, and the water dries up in the pot, but this turns out to be starchy and very heavy.

Mishti Bhat (Sweet Rice)

Ingredients

- 2 cups rice (long grained)
- 4 ½ cups of water
- Half a cup peas
- 3 cloves
- 2 cinnamon sticks
- 4 cardamoms
- 1 tsp full turmeric
- 4 tsp full of oil or 2 tbs of ghee, but ghee is better for taste
- 2 tsp cumin seeds
- ½ cup raisins
- 2 tsp sugar
- half cup split cashew nuts
- Salt to taste

Wash the rice and set aside. Put the ghee/ oil in a wok, add the whole spices and when the ghee/ oil smokes, add the nuts and fry till golden brown. Then add the peas and raisins and sauté for a bit, add the rice and turmeric and sauté for a bit and then pour the mixture in a pot with fitted lid with 4 ½ cups water and let it boil. When it starts boiling, add the salt (about 1 tsp) and the sugar. Put the lid on, lower heat to a minimum and let it cook till the water is absorbed and the rice is cooked. Serve with any vegetable or non-vegetarian curry.

Khichuri (Kejri)

Ingredients

- Equal amount of moong dal and rice (this is for ¾ cup rice and ¾ cup dal)
- 2 onions in quarters
- 3 medium potatoes
- Cauliflower florets of ½ a medium cauliflower
- 2 green chilies, ½ cup peas, 2 chopped tomatoes
- Handful of chopped coriander leaves
- 6 whole cloves
- 4 cardamoms
- 3 cinnamon pieces
- 2 bay leaves
- 3 tsp oil
- 4 tsp ground ginger
- 3 tsp turmeric
- 1½ heaped tsp ground garam masala
- 2 tsp sugar
- 3 tsp ghee/oil
- Salt to taste

Khichuri is a meal by itself. In other states of India, it is made with no spices and given to the ill or elderly. It can also be made with non-vegetarian items such as goat mincemeat, prawns, cubed chicken and cubed goat meat which is pre-cooked and added to the rice.

Fry the dal for ½ min in low heat without any oil and wash it with the rice. Heat oil/ghee in a pressure cooker, put whole cloves, cardamom and cinnamon and bay leaves. Lower the heat and put the rice and dal in and add turmeric, chilies, salt, ginger, sauté everything together till well blended add 4 cups of water, potatoes, and other vegetables i.e., cauliflower etc. Pressure cook for 1 minute. Do not open steam immediately so that it goes on cooking inside.

Other options for vegetables are peas, French beans, cauliflower, carrots, capsicum etc.

Fried Rice With Prawns & Chicken

Ingredients

- 2 cups pan boiled rice.
- 3 chopped onions
- 3 tsp chopped garlic
- ½ cup chopped spring onion
- 4 cloves of chopped garlic
- ¼ cup peas (steamed)
- 1 chopped green chili
- 2 star anise
- 1 ½ tsp curry powder
- 2 tsp soya sauce
- ½ cup shelled pre-cooked prawns and ½ cup dried prawns (pre-soaked)
- 3 tsp fish sauce
- ½ cup boiled shredded chicken
- ¼ cup chopped green capsicums
- 3 tsp sesame oil
- 1 ½ tsp lemon juice

Cook the rice the day before, with the star anise. Soak the dried prawns in ½ cup water. Heat the oil in the wok and when it smokes, fry the onions and garlic and after the onions are pale brown in color, add the vegetables and prawns & chicken and curry powder, sauté a little about half a minute, and then the rice. Stir until mixed thoroughly, add the soya and fish sauce and lemon juice, mix well, and take it of the fire.

Note: The dried prawns should be drained before adding to the rice.

Notes

Dal (Lentils)

Massoor Dal (Red Lentils)

🥣 Ingredients

- 1 cup masur dal
- 4 tsp oil (mustard oil)
- 2 chopped onions
- 1 tsp grated garlic
- 1 heaped tsp turmeric powder
- 2 dry red chili
- 1 tsp full whole jeera
- ½ tsp sugar
- Salt to taste

Wash the dal and pressure cook with 2 ½ cups water. After 1 whistle, turn the heat off as it cooks quickly in a pressure cooker. In a wok, pour in the oil and let it smoke. Lower the heat, add the onions and fry till golden brown, add the other ingredients and fry with 2 tsp full water to prevent the spices from burning, then add the contents into the boiled dal and simmer it till the dal and the spices mix properly. If it is too dry add some water till it is thick and pouring consistency. Turn the heat off.

Arhaar Dal

 Ingredients

- 1 cup arhar dal
- 4 tsp oil (mustard oil)
- 1 ½ tsp of panch phoron - 5 spices (whole) it has methi, saunf, kalonji, mustard seed and whole jeera
- 1 tsp heaped turmeric powder
- 2 tsp of ginger paste
- ½ tsp ground red chili (optional)
- 1 bay leaf
- ½ tsp full hing powder (asafoetida)
- 2 whole dry chilies
- 1 to 2 tsp sugar
- Salt to taste

Pressure cook 1 cup dal in 2 ½ cups water and keep aside. In a frying pan smoke the oil, add all the ingredients except hing. Once it is fried, tip it in the dal and boil until the dal is soft and mushy, add the hing, boil for 1 minute and then take it off the heat.

Cholar Dal (Chana Dal, Split Pea)

Ingredients

- 1 ½ cups chana dal
- 2 grated onions
- 2 tsp garlic paste
- 2 tsp turmeric
- 3 tsp ground ginger
- Whole garam masala of 4 cloves 1 inch cinnamon,4 cardamoms
- 1 tsp garam masala (curry powder)
- 3 chopped tomatoes
- 2 whole dried chilies
- 4 tsp sugar
- ¼ cup raisins
- ½ cup shredded coconut
- Salt to taste

This dal does not increase in volume after cooking and so a little more is required. Boil the dal in 4 cups of water a pressure cooker for 1 minute or so and keep aside. Make sure it is soft and well cooked. In a frying pan smoke the oil and fry the onion, garlic, and sugar till light brown in color, and add all the spices with 2 3 tsp full of water so that it does not burn. Stir and when ready and aromatic, mix with the dal. Mash the dal with the back of the ladle so that it mixes well, and the consistency should not be too thin. Add the coconut and mix well, Turn off the heat.

Karai Dal

Ingredients

- 1 cup karai dal lightly dry sauté on low heat for ½ minute
- 4 tsp oil (mustard oil)
- 3 tsp whole saunf ground
- 2 heaped tsp turmeric powder
- 2 heaped tsp ground ginger
- 2 tsp ground jeera
- 4 green chilies (whole)
- 1 tsp hing powder
- 1 tsp full fresh lemon juice
- Salt to taste

Pressure cook the dal for 1 minute in four cups of water. In a fry pan, smoke the oil and fry the above masala except the ground saunf, hing and lemon juice then pour the masala over the dal and mash the dal with the back of a ladle so that it blends well add lemon juice, ground hing and saunf then boil the dal for a minute to cook the hing and it is ready.

Note: karai dal is perhaps eaten this way only in the eastern region and is supposed to have a distinct flavour and taste of its own. It is eaten with rice and the preferred vegetable to go with it is posto (khuskhus) which is cooked with onion and potatoes or with baigan (brinjal).

Moong Dal

Ingredients

- 1 cup moong dal
- 2 tbsp oil (mustard)
- 2 dry red chilies
- ½ tbsp whole cumin seeds
- 1 tbsp turmeric
- 1 tbsp sugar
- Coriander leaves
- Salt to taste
- In a wok, on medium heat, dry sauté 1 cup dal until pale golden brown. Do not over fry it, take it of the fire and wash the dal. Pressure cook it with 2 ½ cups water and turn off the heat after 1 whistle. In a small frying pan put the oil, chilies, jeera and fry till it starts crackling and fragrant scent of jeera comes on. Put 1 tsp turmeric and pour it over the boiled dal, add the sugar and salt to taste.

Variation: I have given the recipe for plain moong dal but you can add the following: 250 grams of medium sized cauliflower florets cut, 2 tomatoes, 100 grams of peas, 1 tbsp ground fresh ginger.

After cooking the dal you add the above in the oil except the tomatoes, lower the heat and cover the fry pan so that the vegetables are soft and add a little water to cook them. Then add the vegetables and mix it properly with the dal, add the tomatoes and cook till they are soft. You can also add some chopped coriander leaves.

Gota Dal (Lentil With Vegetables)

Ingredients

- 1 cup whole moong lentils soaked for 4-5 hours
- 6 to 8 button baigan
- 6 to 8 broad beans
- 8 small potatoes with skin on
- 8 to 10 whole peas in their pods
- 4 to 5 small spinach plant (or about 100g of whole spinach leaves)
- 2 to 3 whole green chilies
- 3 tsp turmeric
- 3 tsp heaped ginger paste
- 3 tsp heaped coriander powder
- 4 tsp mustard oil
- Salt to taste

This is a wholesome dish which is cooked in January each year on an auspicious day. Wash all the vegetables well and keep aside. Cook the lentils in a pressure cooker until half done and then put all the vegetables and the spices in it and pressure cook enough for the vegetables to be done and well mixed with the lentils. Add the mustard oil on top and serve with rice. You can beat up yoghurt and keep it separately, so that it can be blended into the dal, to give a sour flavor.

Ghugni (Whole Safed Mattar)

Ingredients

- 2 cups safed mattar soaked overnight
- ¾ cup grated coconut
- Whole garam masala of 3 cardamom 3 cinnamons and 4 cloves
- 1 heaped tbsp ground garam masala
- 2 tsp turmeric
- ½ tsp red chili powder
- 1 heaped tbsp fresh ground ginger
- 1 ½ heaped tsp coriander powder
- 1 heaped tsp jeera powder
- 1 tsp whole jeera
- 3 tsp amchur powder
- 3 tsp sugar
- ¼ cup mustard oil
- Salt to taste

Boil the mattar in a pressure cooker with 4 cups of water till soft, about 3 minutes. Then heat the fry pan add the oil to smoke, add the whole garam masala and jeera. Turn down the heat when it splutters, mix the turmeric, ginger, chili powder, coriander powder, jeera powder, amchur powder, salt, sugar and ground garam masala in half cup of water and add to the oil. Turn the heat up, sauté it for a while and then add the mattar and cook it for a further ½ minute until well blended with the masala. Add the grated coconut and mix well. It should have a thick consistency and not too watery. It is served with luchi or on its own.

Vegetables

Charchari (Mixed Vegetable Curry)

🥣 Ingredients

- Total of 6 cups of seasonal vegetables with combination as mentioned in the recipe below
- 3 tsp turmeric powder
- ½ tsp chili powder or to taste
- 3 tsp Panch phoron (whole 5 spices)
- 3 tbsp mustard oil
- Mixed Vegetables
- Salt to taste

Charchari is a generic term in Bengali and means a dry mixed vegetable curry made with seasonal vegetables.

However, there is a choice of vegetables for the curry. The vegetables available in the summer months are never mixed with the ones available in the winter unless the vegetable is available all the year round. The common vegetables all the year around are potatoes, brinjal, kumra (sitaphal) broad beans, potol (parwal), tinda, bitter gourd, lauki, snake gourd (chichinga), mooli (horse radish), seem (broad beans) and a number of edible annual plants. Use equal amount of each vegetables.

Cut the vegetables according to the time each of them takes to cook and is acquired through practice, e.g., for each vegetable to cook from the longest time taken to the least and therefore, the potato size should be half the size of baigan, kumra, and greens should be chopped and put in last.

Heat the wok and put 3 tbsp mustard oil, add 3 tsp of whole 5 spices, dry red chili, and then add the potatoes, fry a little, then add the rest of the vegetables and add turmeric powder chili powder, salt, cover lower heat and let it cook dry. If needed, you may add some water but if greens are added such as spinach, they bring out water and the vegetables cook in it. Make sure that the water dries out completely. So, if there is too much water, turn up the heat and do not cover it. Further, it is better to add the salt last as it brings out water from the vegetable and spinach.

Posto (Opium Seeds, Khuskhus)

🥣 Ingredients

- 80 grams of ground posto (khuskhus)
- 3 medium pealed potatoes and cut in small cubes.
- 2 medium onions cut into small pieces
- 1 slit green chili
- 1 ½ tsp turmeric powder
- 3 tsp mustard oil
- Salt to taste

Put oil in a wok and when it smokes, turn down the heat and add the potatoes and onions and sauté until the potatoes turn a light golden brown, add the turmeric and salt and sauté until the potatoes are coated well. Add 3 quarter cups or 1 cup water cover and cook till the potatoes are tender and the water is about 1/3 cup left in the wok. Add the ground khuskhus slit the chili in half and mix well till the water dries up. This is served with rice and karai dal.

Note: instead of potato you can substitute it with baigan or parwal and the process is the same.

Jhol (Mixed Vegetables With Gravy)

Ingredients

- 3 to 4 cups of vegetables such as parwal (not available in the winter), beans, brinjal, cauliflower, peas, and potatoes
- 4 tbsp of oil (mustard oil)
- 2 heaped tsp ground ginger
- 2 tsp heaped turmeric
- ½ tsp chili
- 1 heaped tsp coriander powder
- 1 tsp of cumin powder
- 1 tsp whole jeera
- 3 medium chopped tomatoes
- Salt to taste

Heat oil in a wok, add whole jeera and once it splutters, add potatoes till it is lightly brown, add the rest of the vegetables except tomatoes and stir occasionally for half a minute and then add the turmeric, ginger, coriander powder, cumin powder and salt with ½ cup of water and sauté everything till well mixed. Add 2 cups water. Cover and cook in low heat for about 5 minutes and add the tomatoes. Turn the heat, off. There should be gravy with the vegetables. This dish is served with rice.

Note: Jhol can be cooked vegetarian or with fish such as rahu, bheckti or prawns. If used, they should be lightly fried and added to the jhol before the tomatoes. Potatoes are not cubed but cut lengthwise with medium sized potato made into 4 pieces and parwal, baigan should also be cut longitudinally. Cauliflower is cut in medium sized florets.

Allur Dom (Dum Alloo)

There are 2 ways to cook Allur Dom.
With hing
Kashmiri dum aloo

🥣 Ingredients for #1 and #2

- 5 medium size potatoes
- 4 tsp of mustard oil
- 1 tsp of whole jeera
- 2 tbsp of coriander ground
- ½ tsp chili powder
- 2 tbsp ginger paste
- 3 tsp of turmeric
- 3 tsp garam masala
- 2 tsp of sugar
- 3 chopped tomatoes
- Corn Starch
- Salt to taste

With hing: pressure cook the potatoes for 1 minute and cool and cut in 4 pieces each. Then heat the oil in a wok, add the jeera, put the sugar, and lower the heat. In half cup water add all the other spices (except hing) and pour it into the oil. Add salt, potatoes and hing and mix well with half a cup of water, cover till the water dries up. If you wish to have gravy, put 1 cup of water and boil till you have the right consistency.

Kashmiri dum aloo: Make it the same way as # 1 method plus add 3 quarter cup beaten yogurt during frying the spices, add hing and the potatoes, and cook until the gravy coats the potatoes use very little water or not at all as yogurt is watery. You might want to beat in ½ tsp of corn starch to the yogurt before adding to the potatoes to make the gravy just coating the potatoes thick.

Laoo (Lauki)

🥣 Ingredients

- 1kg laoo skinned and cut as french fries but thin
- 1 cup grated coconut
- ½ chopped green chili
- 1 bay leaf
- ½ cup peas
- ½ cup milk with half tsp corn starch mixture
- 3 tsp ghee
- 2 tsp sugar
- 1tsp whole cumin seed
- 2 cloves,2 small cardamom and ½ inch cinnamon
- Salt to taste

Laoo comes as a small baseball bat or a round mini football. Peal the skin and cut in french fry pieces. Pressure cook the laoo and peas, After 1 whistle turn off the heat, leave the vegetable in the cooker for 10 minutes, take off the lid and dry out the water. In a wok add the ghee, the whole spices bay leaf and chili to the laoo, then add, salt, sugar, coconut and sauté till well blended, add the milk mixture and dry the water out. Serve with rice.

Note – A great variation is to add 250grams of shrimp to the dish, which you add with the spices.

Baigan Narkol Sarse
(Baigan With Coconut + Sarse)

Ingredients

- 2 medium brinjals
- 1 heaped tsp turmeric
- 3 tbsp mustard seed ground and strained
- 1 chopped green chili
- 1 tsp ground ginger
- 1 tsp kalonji seeds
- ½ cup grated coconut
- 3 tbsp mustard oil + 3 tsp
- Salt to taste

Cut the baigan (brinjal) into medium sized cubes, heat 3 tbsp of mustard oil in a wok, add kalonji and let it splutter. Add the baigan (brinjal), sauté for 1 or 2 minutes with the turmeric and ginger and pour 2 to 3 tbsp water as you go along. Add 3 quarter cups water, cover and simmer till the baigan (brinjals) are soft. Add the green chili, salt, put in the ground mustard and coconut, add the mustard oil and mix everything together till dry and turn off heat. Serve with rice.

Fired Baigan (Brinjal) With Egg

Ingredients

- 2 medium size baigans fired on the gas stove till the skin slides off
- 2 chopped onions
- 1 tsp turmeric
- 2 chopped tomatoes
- ½ chopped green chili
- 1 cup chopped green coriander leaves
- 1 beaten egg
- Salt to taste

In a wok add 1 tsp mustard oil and when it smokes lower the heat, add the onions and fry till golden brown, Chop up the baigan, add them on the onions with the turmeric, tomato, salt and sauté till the mixture is dry. Add the egg on the baigan, and coriander leaves and mix well. Take it off the fire and serve it with rotis.

Sukto (Mixed Vegetables With Bitter Gourd)

Ingredients

- 50 grams potatoes in thick wedges
- 50 grams radish (mooli)
- 50 grams raw banana cut same as radish
- 50 grams broad beans cut in half
- 50 grams cubed sweet potato
- 1 large diced (without the seeds) of bitter gourd
- 8 to 10 boris (they are dried ground lentils as balls that are available in any grocery store)
- 2 tbsp ground mustard seeds
- 5 tsp sugar
- 1 tsp salt
- 1 cubed medium baigan
- 2 tsp corn flour mixed with half cup milk
- 3 tsp ghee
- 4 tbsp mustard oil
- 4 to 3 tsp coriander powder
- 3 tbsp ground ginger

Heat oil and fry the boris and keep aside. In the same oil lightly sauté all the vegetables one by one that is potatoes first and then over it bitter gourd then add the rest of the vegetables, add the ginger, coriander, salt and sugar sauté for 1 minute and then add 1 cup water and pressure cook with 1 whistle as you would cook dal. Open the cooker, When cooled, add mustard and the milk and corn flour and boil once, add the ghee and turn off the heat. If there is less water, add ½ cup water.

Ghonto (Mixed Vegetables With Spinach)

🥣 Ingredients

- 250 grams coarsely cut spinach
- 1 small cauliflower cut into small florets
- 2 medium potatoes cut in small cubes
- ½ cup peas
- 1 white radish cut in cubes
- 1 medium baigan cut in cubes
- ½ cup grated coconut
- 3 tsp of sugar
- 1 tbsp fresh ground ginger
- 4 tsp ground turmeric
- Chili to taste
- 2 tsp ghee
- 4 tsp mustard oil
- 1 tsp whole cumin seeds
- 1 tsp salt

Heat the mustard oil add the cumin seeds and potatoes and then one by one add the other vegetables and sauté for 1 minute, add salt, turmeric, ginger, sugar, chili powder and the spinach. Mix everything together, lower heat and cover and cook till the vegetables are tender. You may need sprinkles of water depending on whether the spinach gives out water or not. If it does, turn the heat high and dry it out by which time the vegetables are soft. Add the grated coconut and the ghee and mix well. Serve with rice.

Palang Sak (Fried Spinach)

Ingredients

- ½ Kg spinach cut fine
- 1 tsp whole 5 spices
- 2 tsp of mustard oil
- 1 dry red chili
- Salt to taste

Heat the oil in a wok and when it smokes, put the red chili and 5 spices, lower heat, add the spinach, and cook till the water dries out. Add salt and take it off the heat. Serve with rice.

Mocha (Banana Flower)

Ingredients

- 1 mocha peeled and flower taken out
- 2 medium potatoes cubed very small
- 1 heaped tbsp ground ginger
- 2 tsp turmeric powder + 2 tsp
- 2 tsp coriander powder
- Chili to taste
- 4 tsp sugar
- 2 tsp oil
- 2 tsp of ghee
- ½ cup coconut grated
- 1 tsp salt + 1tsp

The banana flower is conical in shape and covered with coarse petals. If you open each petal of the flower, you will find each flower has stamens and a pistil in the center. Take the pistil out and throw it away. You will also find a single opaque leaf which is white in color, you need to take that out as well. Once all the flowers are done and there are no more maroon petals that you can take out, cut up the conic structure and cut finely with the flowers. Pressure cook the cut flower in turmeric and salt, and then strain the water. Heat oil and jeera in a wok, fry the potatoes till half tender, add turmeric, coriander, ginger, salt and sugar, flower sprinkle water and sauté everything. Lastly, add coconut and the ghee and mix them well. Turn off the heat.

Kanthal (Raw Jack Fruit)

🥣 Ingredients

- 750 grams kanthal peeled and cubed
- 2 tsp 5 spices
- 3 tsp sugar
- 3 tsp turmeric powder +1tsp
- 2 tsp cumin powder
- 3 tsp coriander powder
- 1 heaped tsp ground garam masala
- 2 heaped tsp fresh ground ginger
- Chili powder to taste
- 1 tsp hing powder
- 3 to 4 chopped tomatoes
- 1 ½ heaped tsp amchur powder
- 3 to 4 medium cubed potatoes
- 3 tbsp mustard oil
- Salt to taste +1tsp

Mix 1 tsp haldi + 1 tsp salt with the kanthal. Pressure cook the kanthal and throw out the water. Heat oil put the whole spices the potatoes, sauté until light brown then add the rest of the spices adding sprinkling of water in between. Add 1 cup water, cover and cook 2 min Add the kanthal and sauté tomatoes, salt, sugar, hing and cook until there is a small amount of gravy.

Note: Nowadays the whole raw jack fruit is available in the market, cleaned and cut into pieces but they do not take out the thick white covering over the seed so, slice the seed and throw away the hard covering. The pieces should be 1-2 inch cubed.

Kumra Potol (Pumpkin With Palwal Chakka)

Ingredients

- ½ kg pumpkin cut in cubes
- 250 grams of palwal peeled, cut and seeds taken out and then diced into thick pieces
- 2 to 3 medium potatoes cubed
- 2 tsp panch phoron (five spice)
- ½ tsp chili powder
- 1 heaped tbsp ground ginger
- 1 tbsp garam masala powder
- 3 tsp dhania powder
- 1 tsp hing
- 3 tsp sugar
- 1 heaped tsp amchur powder
- 2 tbsp mustard oil
- 2 tsp salt

Heat the oil in a wok, add the potatoes and parwal, and sauté till light brown, and last add the pumpkin, sauté for a bit. Once it becomes light golden colour, put all the spices except amchur and hing. Sprinkle water to the spices and vegetables, then add 3 quarter cup water, cover and simmer till the water dries up. Add amchur and hing and mix well. It can be served with rice and all Indian breads.

Kochur Sak (Cholocasium Plant)

Ingredients

- 1kg long stem of kochur sak
- 3 heaped tsp ground ginger
- ½ tsp whole cumin seeds
- 2 tsp sugar
- 2 tsp mustard oil
- ½ cup grated coconut
- ½ tsp salt

Cut the stem of the plant in 2-inch pieces but before doing that slice off strings along the length of the leaves and throw them out. Boil the cut stem in 2 cups water in a pressure for a minute after the whistle. Leave it to cool. When it is done, strain the contents and squeeze out excess water completely. Heat the oil in a wok, when it smokes turn down the heat, add the cumin and ground ginger and put the mashed stem in, add the salt and sugar add the coconut, sauté till everything is mixed and turn off the heat. Serve with rice.

Bhindi Sharse (Okhra With Mustard)

Ingredients

- 400 grams bhindi
- 3 tsp turmeric
- ¼ cup ground and strained mustard with a little water
- 2 tbsp + 1 tbsp mustard oil
- Chili powder to taste
- ½ cup beaten yogurt
- Salt to taste

In this recipe it is important to buy soft and small bhindi, Tip and tail them i.e., cut the head and end off before washing, since washing them after cutting gives off a slimy liquid which is undesirable. If the bhindi is too large, cut them in two pieces (avoid large and ripe ones).

Heat the 2 tbsp oil in a wok till it smokes, lower the heat and fry the bhindi for a min, add the turmeric and sauté until the bhindi is well coated with the turmeric, add chili powder and a cup of water. Cover and cook till the vegetable is soft and the water dries up. Add the mustard and yogurt and 1tbsp oil, and then the salt. Mix everything together.

Note – Bhindi cooks well in a microwave, so you can reduce the water to ¼ cup and cover and cook it at high for 5-7 minutes, add the yogurt, mustard and oil and finish in a wok.

Chanar Kofta (Cottage Cheese/ Paneer Ball Curry)

🥣 Ingredients

- 2 tbsp milk (full fat)/ or 300 grams of cottage cheese
- 2 tbsp vinegar
- 2 tsp turmeric
- 1 heaped tbsp ginger ground
- 1 tsp ground cumin
- 3 tsp ground coriander
- 2-3 tsp sugar
- 1 tsp ground garam masala
- 2 chopped tomatoes
- 1 tsp whole cumin
- 4 tsp corn flour
- ½ cup mustard oil
- Salt to taste ½ tsp

Boil the milk in a saucepan. Mix the vinegar and ¼ cup water and once the milk starts to boil lower the heat and pour the vinegar in a slow stream, stirring constantly and soon the milk will curdle. Once the water is clear and the cheese separates, turn the heat off and keep it for 5 minutes. Then strain the cheese, squeeze till all the water is out. Instead of this, you might buy cottage cheese from a store.

Put the chana in a blender till it is smooth with ½ tsp of salt. Sprinkle the corn flour and mix well and then make balls the size of a small potato (or a little bigger) and shallow fry two/ three of them at a time in ¼ cup hot oil until golden brown. Make sure they do not color dark brown.

In the wok, pour more oil if necessary (about 2 tbsp), lower heat, add all the spices in a little water and fry them on low heat for about ½ a minute. Once the oil separates from the spices, pour 1 cup of water and once it simmers, gently put all the balls in. Simmer for 15 seconds or and turn off the heat.

Beguner Raita (Brinjal With Yogurt)

Ingredients

> - 1 large or 2 medium brinjals
> - 1 cup mustard oil
> - 2 tsp salt + 1 tsp
> - 1 heaped tsp turmeric
> - 1 tsp sugar
> - 1 cup beaten yogurt
> - 2 medium chopped onions
> - 1 hand full of chopped coriander leaves
> - 2 tsp ground cumin
> - 1 chopped green chili
> - 2 tsp mustard powder

Slice off the head and bottom of the baigan and make 1-inch slice of a large brinjal and cut each slice to make 2 half-moons per slice. For the medium ones, slice of the ends and also do the same. You will probably have 8-10 half moon pieces for each of the sizes.

Smoke the oil in a wok, and smear turmeric and 2 tsp salt on the brinjals. Fry on both sides (4 pieces at a time) to a golden color under medium heat and put them on kitchen paper to absorb excess oil. Place them on a flat dish. Mix the salt, sugar, mustard powder and cumin with the beaten yogurt and pour it evenly over all the brinjal pieces. Sprinkle the onions on top and then the coriander. It is normally served with any unleavened bread.

Dhokar Dalna

Ingredients

- 1 cup channa dal (split yellow dal)
- 1 cup mustard oil
- 1 heaped tsp cumin powder
- 1 heaped tsp kalonji (onion seeds)
- 3 heaped tsp coriander powder
- 1 heaped tbsp ginger paste
- 4 tsp turmeric powder
- Chili to taste
- 4 tsp sugar
- 2 heaped tsp ground garam masala
- 3 medium chopped tomatoes
- 1 tsp amchur powder
- 1 tsp hing powder
- 1 tsp enos fruit salt or ½ tsp sodium bicarbonate
- Salt to taste + 1 tsp

Soak the dal overnight and grind it to a paste (not too much water) with 1 tsp salt. Put a 12-inch pot (which has a lid with about 1½ - 2-inch rise on the edge like a pie pan but in steel foil that sits on the pan of boiling water – (it is like a steamer with no holes). Set the water boil to add the soda to the dal and quickly spread the ground dal evenly in the pan. Cover with another cover or you could use a double cover of tin foil. Steam for 20 minutes and turn the heat off.

Let the ground lentils cool a bit and then cut them in squares, about 1½ - 2 inch each.

Heat ¾ cup of oil in a wok and fry the squares in batches till they are golden brown in color. Heat 3 tbsp oil in the wok. Mix all the spices except the hing and sauté till the mixture is light brown in color and aromatic. Add 2-2½ cups of water and when the gravy starts to boil put the hing and gently put the fried lentil squares in, making sure they do not break. When there is 2 cups of gravy, turn off the heat.

Beet Chop (Beetroot Croquete)

Ingredients

- 4 large beets
- 2 medium potatoes
- ¾ cup shelled peas
- 2 tbsp ground ginger
- 2 medium onions
- 2 heaped tsp garam masala
- Chilli to taste
- Handful of coriander leaves
- 2 tsp cumin powder
- 2 tsp sugar
- Batter made of water and flour (not too thick or runny)
- 1 cup mustard oil + 1 tsp
- Bread crumbs
- Salt to taste

Peel and cut the beets into very small pieces, and also the potato, peas and onions. Heat 1 tbsp oil and fry the onions and potatoes till golden brown and add the spices, beets, potatoes, add coriander and add a sprinkle of water. Cover and cook for a minute on low heat stirring occasionally. Once it is dry but can bind into egg-shaped balls turn off the heat. In a wok pour oil and while it heats, dip the balls in the batter and roll them into the breadcrumbs. When the oil smokes, turn down the heat and fry the balls, 3-4 at a time till they are golden brown. Add more oil if necessary. Take them out and when done put them on kitchen paper to drain the extra oil.

Soups

Mattar Soup With Pudina (Pea Soup With Mint)

Ingredients

- 2 cups shelled peas
- 2 cups water
- 1 tsp corn flour
- 1 cup milk
- ¼ cup cream
- Salt to taste
- 1 tsp sugar
- 2 tsp chopped mint

Pressure-cook the peas in the water for 1-2 minutes and then drain the water. Keep the water and add milk and corn flour. Blend thoroughly and put it on boil. Add 2 tsp corn flour, salt, sugar, and freshly ground black pepper – watch the heat as it may boil over. When it is soup consistency, turn off the heat and add the cream and chopped mint.

Brocolli Soup With Cheese

Ingredients

- 1 broccoli cut into pieces
- 2 cups water
- ½ tsp salt
- ½ glass milk
- ¼ cup cream
- ¼ cup stilton/cheddar (grated)

Boil 1 broccoli without the stems in 2 cups water and follow exactly the pea soup process. Do not use corn flour and finally add the cream and ¼ cup of stilton or any hard cheese as cheddar.

Mulligatawny (Lentil)

🥣 Ingredients

- ¾ cup red lentils
- ¾ cups water
- 3 chopped onion
- 3 tsp garlic paste
- 1 bay leaf
- 3 tsp coriander powder
- 1 tbsp butter
- 1 tsp corn flour
- Juice of 1 lemon
- 2 cups chicken broth or 2 chicken soup cubes
- Salt to taste

Mulligatawny is an Anglo-Indian soup founded by the cooks in the south of India. Put all ingredients in 3 cups of water. Pressure-cook for 2 minutes. Once done, take out the bay leaf, and boil with 2 cups of chicken broth or 2 soup cubes, salt, pepper, and 1 tsp corn flour to make it a smooth consistency. Add the butter and the juice of 1 lemon (2 tbsp or so) to give it a pungent taste.

Minestrone (Tomato)

Ingredients

- 6 large tomatoes
- 1 large, grated onion
- 1 peeled and chopped carrot
- 1 tsp garlic paste
- 1 cup chicken broth or 2 chicken soup cubes
- Shredded chicken, about ¾ cup
- Left over rice, if any, or ½ cup pasta
- 3 tsp olive oil
- 2 tsp oregano or Italian herbs
- ½ cup grated parmesan/ cheddar cheese
- Salt and pepper to taste

Minestrone is an Italian soup. Boil the tomatoes in 1½ cups of water just to allow the skin to peel off. Blend it in the blender and keep aside. In a pan, add the onion, garlic, carrot, and chicken and sauté for a bit on high heat. Add the chicken broth, tomato puree and all the other ingredients until the soup is about 6-7 cups. Before serving, add the cheese. Use ½ tsp of corn flour if required.

Pyaz Soup (French Onion)

Ingredients

- 4 large onions chopped
- 3 tsp white oil
- 1 tsp sugar
- 4 cup chicken broth or 2 mutton chicken soup cubes boiled in 4 cups water
- Cubed bread (4 cubes per person fried in 2 tbsp oil)
- ½ cup grated parmesan cheese
- 1 tsp pepper
- 1 tsp salt

Fry onions in oil, add sugar to brown the onion, when light brown, add chicken broth or mutton cubes and boil it with a cup of water, add salt and pepper while it is boiling. Add 4 cubes of fried bread per bowl. Put the soup over the bread and garnish with parmesan cheese (3 tsp in each bowl). Serve rusk as a shortcut instead of fried bread.

Beet (Bortch)

Ingredients

- 4 beetroots
- 1 tsp sugar
- ½ cup cream
- ½ tsp corn flour
- ½ glass milk
- ½ tsp salt

This is originally a Russian soup and is best served chilled. Boil in a pressure cooker 4 beetroots for 30-40 minutes, peel skin, liquidize and boil for 2 minutes with 1 glass water, milk, salt, sugar, cream and corn flour. Chill and serve. A lighter option is not to use cream but mix 2 cups of milk and 2 tsp corn flour instead.

Gajjar (Carrot With Orange)

Ingredients

- ½ kg carrot, peeled and diced
- ½ cup beaten yoghurt
- 2 tsp butter (optional)
- 2 tsp sugar
- ½ tsp pepper
- 1 tsp corn starch
- ½ cup milk
- ½ cup orange juice

Boil ½ kg carrots in 3 cup water and add when it thickens, liquidize, add beaten yoghurt, salt, sugar, black pepper to taste. Mix corn starch and milk and add. When it thickens, take it off the fire and add orange juice. Adding butter is optional.

Bhutta Soup (Corn Soup)

Ingredients

- 100 grams of shredded chicken, prawn, or crab
- 2 tins of sweet corn or 5 corns on the cob
- 2 chicken soup cube
- 1 large glass or 1½ medium glass of water
- 1 tsp corn starch
- 1½ tsp dark soya sauce
- 2 tsp of vinegar
- 1 chopped green chili
- 1 beaten egg
- 2 tsp sesame or peanut oil
- Salt and pepper to taste

If using fresh corn, slice the corn off the cob and pressure cook for 2 minutes with 2 to 3 cups of water. Keep the water, mash the corn with the back of a ladle. If using tinned corn, in both cases, put all ingredients in a pan except the egg. Boil the corn for 3-4 minutes and add the egg in a stream so that it makes small segments in the soup. It should not have a thin consistency, if so add a little more corn starch (1 tsp). Turn off the heat after one minute.

Notes

Fish

The west Bengalis rarely eat sea fish. Sea fish have this strong fishy smell which is not desirable. The Bengalis who settle abroad make do with cod and haddock. Salmon and trout are river fishes which are available but expensive.

In west Bengal there are very similar tasting fish like the trout, parshe, tangra, pabda, topshe to name a few that are different from each other and their own distinguished flavor but do not grow beyond 10 inches to 12 inches in length unlike rahu and bheckti which can be anywhere between 1kg and 12kgs. Mural fish that are 2 to 3 inches long can be compared to white bait and are used for deep frying and served crispy or cooked like a chutney.

Therefore, variation in cooking fish is endless by the Bengali. Lobsters, prawns and the humble shrimp are all time favorites.

Mach With Sarse (Mustard Fish)

 Ingredients

- 750 grams of rahu/carp/salmon/bheckti
- 1 tsp salt
- 1 ½ tsp turmeric +1 tsp
- ½ tsp of chilies
- 2 slit green chilies half
- ¼ cup ground and strained mustard seeds
- ½ cup mustard oil
- ½ cup beaten yoghurt
- Salt to taste

Cut the fish in 2 to 3inch squares. Smear with 1 tsp of salt and 1 ½ tsp of turmeric. Put oil in a wide base fry pan and when the oil smokes, reduce heat, and place the pieces very gently and fry them until light brown on both sides. Mix 1½ tsp of turmeric, chili powder in half cup water and pour it on the fish, add another ½ cup water, 2 slit green chilies and cook the fish for a minute. Mix ½ cup yoghurt, the strained ground mustard and pour the yoghurt mixture and take it off the fire, when the gravy starts to boil. Serve with rice.

Dahi Mach (Fish Cooked In Yoghurt)

Ingredients

- 750 grams river fish cut in piece
- ½ cup dahi (yoghurt) thick consistency
- 3 green chilies cut up in 3 to 4 per each
- 1 + 1 tsp turmeric
- 2 tsp sugar
- Whole spices of 4 cloves, 3 cardamoms, 2 cinnamon stick
- 2 tbsp white oil or ghee
- 1 tbsp heaped ginger paste
- 1½ + ½ tsp salt

Wash the fish and marinate in 1 tsp turmeric and 1½ tsp salt for 10 minutes. Put the oil/ghee in the wok and smoke it, lower the heat and place all the fish in the oil, stirring constantly until the oil/ghee coats all the fish and take the pieces out on a plate. Do not fry the fish. Just sauté it in the oil/ ghee.

Beat the yoghurt well and keep aside, mix the salt, sugar, chili, whole spices ginger paste in 1 cup of water and pour over the fish. Cover, and simmer for about 2 minutes, add a little water if too dry, add the yoghurt & simmer. The gravy should be a little thick, Turn off the heat.

Maccher Ghonto (Fish With Vegetables)

Ingredients

- 250 grams of cubed fish (rahu, bheckti, salmon or singhara
- 2 cups of small cauliflower florets
- ½ medium baigan cut in 1inch cubes
- 1 large chopped onion
- 2 medium potatoes cut in half inch cubed pieces
- ½ cup tsp of mustard oil
- 1 heaped tsp garam masala powder
- Whole garam masala of 4 cloves, 2 cinnamon sticks and 4 cardamoms
- 3 tsp sugar
- 1 heaped tsp garlic paste
- 2 tsp of turmeric + ½ tsp
- 2 tsp of ground ginger
- Chili powder to taste
- Salt to taste + 1 tsp

Smear the fish with 1 tsp turmeric and 1 tsp salt and keep aside. Fry the fish lightly and set aside. Gently take the fish bones out. In the same oil add the whole garam masala, sugar, garlic, onions until light brown, add the ginger and ground garam masala, add the potatoes and all the vegetables and sauté stirring all the time, add the fish and sauté till the fish crumbles and mixes with the vegetables, add salt and carry on cooking adding ½ cup of water till it is completely dry.

Maccher Muri Ghonto (Beaten Rice With Fish/ Fish Head)

Ingredients

- 500 grams of fish (rahu, salmon, bheckti or singhara)
- 2 cups of flattened rice
- 4 cloves, 2 stick cinnamon, 4 cardamoms
- 2 + 1 tsp turmeric powder
- 1 heaped tbsp ginger paste
- ½ tsp cumin powder
- 1 tsp whole spices
- 2 medium onions sliced
- 4 tsp ground garlic
- 2 tsp sugar
- ¼ cup mustard oil
- Salt to taste +1 tsp

Cut the fish into 2 to 3inch pieces and smear with 1 tsp turmeric and 1 tsp salt. Soak the beaten rice in 2 to 3 cups water to wash the starch out. Strain the water out.

In a wok put the oil, let it smoke, lower heat, add the onion and garlic and put in the fish. Sauté it till it turns into golden brown color and take it out of the oil. Put the rest of spices in the same oil and sauté for 1 to 2 minutes, add the beaten rice, mix everything together. Now put back the fish, add salt and sauté the fish and the beaten rice for 2 minutes and take it off the heat. Sprinkle water, if necessary,

Note: the name of the dish is called moori ghonto, moori meaning puffed rice but raw flattered rice is used which is called chinre in Bengal.

Maccher Roast (Fish Roast)

Ingredients

- 1 large rahu fish (7-8 kg) – from which 4 pieces of 150 grams each
- 3 grated medium onions
- 1 tbsp ground garlic
- 1 heaped tbsp ground ginger
- 2 tsp turmeric
- 1 tsp garam masala
- 2 tbsp white oil
- 1 tsp sugar
- Salt to taste

This recipe is from the cooks of the British Raj. The choice of rahu fish is to ensure fewer bones. Smoke the oil in a wok and put the onions, garlic and turmeric, garam masala, salt and sugar. Place the fish pieces gently in the wok and smear the pieces with the onion mixture. Turn the heat off and keep it covered for two hours to marinate. Line a baking tray with tin foil and bake the fish in the oven at 180 degrees Celsius for 10 minutes on each side. Test the fish with a fork to ensure that it is cooked through. If not, keep it in for another 5-7 minutes. Make sure it doesn't burn.

Chingri Sarse/ Bati Charchari (Prawn Mustard)

🥣 Ingredients

- 500 grams of medium prawns (with head on or off)
- ¼ tsp mustard seeds ground to a paste and strained with ¼ cup of water
- 2 tsp turmeric powder
- 2 green chilies broken in half
- Salt to taste
- ¼ cup thick yoghurt, hung to take the water out
- 2 tbsp mustard oil

Mix all the spices, oil, and the strained mustard seed paste in a bowl, and smear the fish. Cover and steam it in a pressure cooker for 3 minutes, take it off the heat and add the yoghurt, simmer for another 1 minute or so, turn off heat, serve with rice.

Chingri Malai Curry (Prawn With Coconut Milk)

Ingredients

- 700 grams of medium or large prawns (keep the heads on for taste and we love chewing them)
- 1 ½ cup coconut milk (best way is to grate ½ coconut and put it in a blender with hot water and soak it for 10 minutes). Strain the milk or you can use canned coconut milk (1 cup)
- 2 cardamoms, 3 cloves. 1 inch cinnamon and 1 bay leaf
- 1 tsp turmeric powder
- 1 onion grated, 3 tsp ginger paste
- 1 tbsp garlic paste
- Chili powder to taste
- 2 tsp sugar
- 1 tbsp ghee or oil
- ½ tsp corn flour mixed with ¼ cup milk
- Salt to taste

Put the prawns in a bowl and marinate them with the coconut milk for 2 to 3 hours.

Heat the ghee/oil and put the whole spices sauté a bit, add the garlic, onion, ginger, turmeric, salt and sugar and sauté till well blended, add the prawn with the coconut milk simmer till there is 1 cup gravy. Then add the corn flour milk, simmer until the sauce thickens. Turn off the heat.

Macher Ombol (Hot + Sour Fish Chutney)

Ingredients

- 250 grams of small whole fish of your choice
- 2 tbsp mustard oil
- 1 tbsp imli paste (tamarind)
- 1 tbsp ground gur (jaggery)
- 1 ½ tsp turmeric + ½ tsp
- 1 tsp ground garlic
- 1 tsp ground ginger
- Salt to taste + ½ tsp

One can use mourala (white bait) for this recipe, but any other similar kind or small river fish will do. Smear the fish with ½ tsp turmeric and ½ tsp salt and keep aside. Heat the oil in a wok and once it smokes, lower the heat, and sauté the fish for a minute, add the garlic, turmeric, ginger, salt, jaggery, and imli paste. Sauté with a sprinkle of water, and once everything is blended pour 1 cup of water, cover and simmer until a little gravy is left. Turn off the heat. This goes well with rice.

Bheckti Pathuri (Bheckti Fish Wrapped In Banana Leaf)

Ingredients

- Banana leaf (6pcs of "8*8" square)
- Bheckti fish (6 pcs of 50 grams each)
- 2 tbsp heaped mustard seed (ground to a paste)
- 1 tsp turmeric powder
- 6 green chilies
- 1 tsp heaped ginger paste
- 2 tbsp mustard oil
- Thread
- Salt to taste

This fish recipe is a delicacy in Bengal and the authentic quality is with Bheckti fish which is a river fish (not sea Bheckti) which is longer in size and has a very strong smell. Bengalis do not eat this variety.

Take the banana leaves and pass them through the fire to soften each one for 15 secs and the thick central vein of the leaf. Mix the mustard, turmeric, ginger, salt, and oil to a paste and divide it into 6 portions and mix each portion of the gravy with each piece of fish and place each fish in the center of the leaf, put the green chili broken into pieces in each of the fish. Then wrap the fish up in a neat packet and tie it with string properly.

Place all the packets in a steamer for about 20 minutes or bake in an oven at 180 degree for 10 minutes. Open the packet and serve the fish with rice. This recipe could be done using Rahu fish, if Bheckti is not available.

Maccher Jhol (Fish Jhol With Gravy)

Ingredients

- Any river fish (Rahu, Bheckti) – 400 grams cut in pieces of approximately 50 grams each
- 2 tsp turmeric + 1 tsp
- 2 tbsp ground ginger
- 1 tbsp coriander
- 1 green chili cut in 3 pieces
- 1 tomato cut in pieces
- ½ cup mustard oil
- 1 tsp whole cumin seeds
- 2 medium potatoes cut in long fat pieces
- 6-8 medium florets of cauliflower
- 6-8 medium pieces of brinjal cut into 3 by 2 inch pieces
- ½ cup peas
- Salt to taste

Clean the fish and marinate it well with 1 tsp turmeric and 1 tsp salt and put aside for 10 minutes. Put oil in a wok and smoke it, turn the heat to medium and put pieces of fish one at a time and gently fry it on both sides. When all the pieces are done put all the vegetables in the same oil and sauté for ½ a minute. Add the spices in the same oil, lower the heat. Add ¾ cup water and when it boils add the fish pieces gently to avoid breaking add green chili and simmer it for 2 minutes on medium heat till a little gravy is left.

Maccher Mathar Daal – Moong Or Chana Dal (Fish Head With Lentils)

Very daunting for non-Bengalis to hear the name of this recipe let alone cook and eat it but believe me the taste is out of this world. If you are squeamish about fish heads, I recommend using rahu fish cut in pieces instead.

Ingredients

- 750 grams of fish head broken into 3 to 4 pieces by the fish monger or 500grams of rahu fish cut in 2*2inch pieces
- 1 cup moong dal or 1 ½ cup chana dal
- 1 heaped tbsp ground garlic
- 2 heaped tbsp ground ginger
- 2 medium grated onions
- 1 tsp turmeric + 1 tbsp
- 3 cloves
- 2 inch cinnamon stick
- 3 cardamoms
- 2 tsp whole cumin seeds
- 1 bay leaf
- 3 tsp sugar
- ½ tsp chili powder
- 2 tsp heaped garam masala powder
- 2 to 3 medium chopped tomatoes
- ¾ cup mustard oil
- Salt ½ tsp + 1 tsp

Rub the fish head/fish pieces with 1 tsp turmeric and ½ tsp salt and fry in a very hot oil and keep aside. In another wok dry fry the moong dal and pressure cook it with 3 cups water; just 1 whistle. In case of chana dal do not fry it but pressure cook it for 1 to 2 minutes until soft. In the oil left in the wok, fry the onion and garlic, and then add all the spices with quarter cup water till the oil separates from the masala. Pour in the dal and the fish and simmer with 1 cup water for 2 or 3 minutes until the consistency is thick and not watery. Serve it hot with rice.

Macher Kalia (Fish With Potatoes)

 Ingredients

- 750g of rahu (carp) cut into 2*3 pieces
- 4 medium potatoes made into 8 pieces
- 3 medium grated onions
- 3 tsp turmeric + 2 tsp
- 3 heaped tsp garlic paste
- 2 heaped tsp cumin seeds
- Whole spices (4 cardamoms, 4 cloves and 2 cinnamon stick)
- 1 tsp chili powder
- 3 tsp sugar
- ¾ cup mustard oil
- 2 or 3 chopped tomatoes
- Salt to taste + 1 tsp

Smear the fish pieces with 1 tsp salt and 2 tsp turmeric. Heat the oil in the wok and when it smokes, reduce heat to medium and fry the fish 3 at a time till they are golden color on both sides; take them out. In the same oil fry the potatoes until light brown, then add the whole spices, onion, garlic, cumin, and all the other ingredients in quarter cup water and sauté in low heat till the mixture is well done, add the tomatoes, and put 2 cups water cover and cook for 2-3 minutes till the potatoes are tender, then add the fish, add a little water if necessary. Once the gravy is thick and the fish is done, take it off the heat.

Macher Chop (Fish Croquettes)

Ingredients

- 300 grams of rahu fish
- 4 large potatoes
- 2 medium sliced onions
- 1 heaped tsp of garlic paste
- ½ tsp chili powder
- whole spice (4 cloves, 2 sticks cinnamon, 3 cardamoms)
- 1 tsp sugar
- Salt to taste + ½ tsp salt for the potatoes
- 1 cup of mustard oil for frying
- 1½ tsp or turmeric

Thin batter made out of flour and water, enough to coat the fish
1 cup breadcrumbs

Cut the fish into 4 pieces and boil for 2 minutes in water. Strain the water and mash them roughly making sure there are no bones. Boil and peel the potatoes and mash them while they are hot until there are no lumps.

Heat a wok, pour 2 tsp oil and when it smokes, put the spices in and sauté for 1 minute, then put the mashed fish and sauté till everything is mixed and the fish is dry, enough to make small balls.

Then put some salt in the potatoes, about ½ tsp and make even sized balls the size of medium onion. With fingers make a cup of each ball and put a ball of the fish mixture into the potato cup and seal it into a round ball which should be the size of a duck egg. Make all this size with the potato and fish. Then make a batter of flour and water and drop each one in it and roll it in breadcrumbs.

Heat the oil in the wok and fry 3-4 at a time to a golden-brown color. Place each croquette in paper towels to absorb the excess oil. Serve hot with tomato sauce.

NOTE: - In the same way you can make vegetable croquettes with peas. Blend 3 cup peas in a blender and make the stuffing as for fish croquettes without the onion and garlic. But add ½ tsp sugar and 1 tsp cumin seeds. Everything else is the same as in the recipe.

Lau Chingri (Gourd With Shrimp)

🥣 Ingredients

- 750g of lau, peeled and cut into small French fries' size
- 250g of shrimps
- Whole spices (1cinnamon, 2cardomoms, and 4cloves)
- 1 medium potato cut in small cubes
- 1 tsp turmeric + 1 tsp
- 2 tsp ground ginger
- 1 ½ tsp ground garlic
- ½ tsp chili powder
- 1 tsp corn flour
- ¼ cup water
- 2 tsp sugar
- 1 tsp whole cumin
- 4 tsp ghee/oil
- Salt to taste

Pressure cook the lauki with ½ cup water and take it off the fire after one whistle. In a wok put the ghee and the whole spices and cumin, fry for a bit, add the garlic, turmeric, chili powder and ginger, put in the prawns (pre-smeared with 1tsp turmeric) and sauté for a bit, put the salt and sugar. Dry the water from the lauki and put it in the wok and sauté everything together till well mixed. Add ¼ cup water mixed with 1 tsp corn flour and sauté till it dries up. It is served with rice.

Macher Fry (Fried Fish)

Ingredients

- 400g of sliced bheckti fish (about 4 inch * 3 inch * 6mm thick)
- 1 grated onion
- 2 tsp ground garlic
- 2 heaped tsp ginger paste
- 1 tsp chopped chilies
- ¾ cup mustard oil
- 1 cup of flour batter/2 eggs beaten
- 1 cup breadcrumbs
- 1 tsp lemon juice
- Salt to taste

Mis the spices together and the salt and marinate the fish in this mixture for 2 hours. Take each piece, coated with spices and dip into the flour batter egg and cover it with the breadcrumbs thoroughly by pressing the crumbed fish pieces. Heat a wide based fry pan, with the oil and, as it smokes, lower the heat and fry them till golden brown on both sides. Fry 3-4 pieces at a time and when done, place on a paper towel to remove excess oil. Serve with mustard paste.

Notes

Meat
(Mutton and Chicken)

Mangshor Jhol (Goat Meat Curry)

Ingredients

- 750 grams of de-boned goat meat
- 4 medium sized potatoes peeled and halved
- 1 heaped tsp turmeric
- 2 heaped tbs ground ginger
- 3 grated onions
- 1 heaped tbsp garlic
- Salt to taste
- 1 tsp chili powder
- 2 heaped tsp ground garam masala
- 4 tbs mustard oil
- 4 tsp vinegar
- 4 cloves, 2sticks cinnamon and 4 cardamom, 2 bay leaves
- 2 tsp sugar

In a wok smoke the oil. Fry the onions and garlic and potatoes, add salt and sugar, ginger, turmeric and chili powder with ½ cup water and sauté till brown in color. Tip the lot into the pressure cooker add 1 cup water and the meat and pressure cook on low heat for 25 minutes, allow pressure to release automatically. If the gravy dries up, add another ½ cup water and boil till there is gravy left with the meat.

Goat Meat Pulao (Mutton Pulao)

🥣 Ingredients

- 2 cups basmati rice
- 750gm cubed mutton (boneless)
- 5 medium potatoes halved
- 4 tsp garlic
- 2 heaped tbs ginger (ground)
- Chili powder to taste
- whole garam masala (4 cloves, 4 cardamoms, 2 sticks of cinnamon)
- 2 bay leaves
- ½ tsp saffron soaked in half cup warmed milk.
- 3 tbsp rose water
- 1 cup beaten yoghurt
- 2 tsp whole cumin seed
- 4 tbsp ghee (clarified butter) or oil and butter combination
- salt and pepper to taste

The best taste comes out using mutton but chicken can be used. Put the meat in a pressure cooker and mix all the ingredients well except the saffron, ghee and rose water. Cook for 25 minutes. Take out the pieces of meat in a pan with a fitted lid and keep aside after sieving the liquid.

In a wok put the ghee/ butter and add the washed rice and sauté for 1 minute over low heat with the potatoes. Measure the liquid and top it with total 4 ½ cups of water. Pour this over the meat and rice and add the saffron milk, rosewater and cook as you would cook rice, that may be 2 minutes after the whistle goes and then turn of the heat. If you use chicken, reduce the cooking time to 10 minutes instead of 25 minutes for goat meat. The rest of the process is the same.

Sada Mangsho (White Color Goat Meat Curry)

Ingredients

- 750 grams of boneless mutton cubed
- 2 cups beaten yoghurt mixed with 1 tsp corn flour
- 3 heaped tsp ginger
- 2 tsp garlic
- 4 cloves,3 cardamoms and 2inch cinnamon
- 4 slit green chilies
- 25 grams of chopped coriander leaves
- 1 heaped tsp garam masala
- 2 to 3 medium onions sliced and fried in 3 tsp white oil till brown
- 2 tbsp full of ghee
- 1tsp full sugar
- Quarter cup ground cashew nut and quarter cup ground almonds
- Salt to taste

Soak the mutton in the yoghurt, ginger, salt, sugar and leave it overnight. Next day pressure cook it for 20 minutes and keep aside. In a wok add the ghee and the garlic fry it a little and pour it over the meat. Add the yoghurt and the chopped coriander leaves. Add the cashew nut paste and almond paste, mix everything together and take it off the heat and add the fried onions on top.

Mangsho Palang Sak (Goat Meat With Spinach)

Ingredients

- 750 grams of mutton (cubed)
- 3 grated onions
- 3 tsp garlic paste
- 3 tsp turmeric
- 2 heaped tsp ginger paste
- 3 tsp ground garam masala
- 4 cardamoms, 2 cinnamon, 6 cloves
- 4 tbsp mustard oil
- 3 chopped tomatoes
- 1 cup chopped coriander leaves
- 400 grams of chopped spinach or 500 grams of frozen spinach
- Salt to taste

Pressure-cook the mutton for 25 minutes and put it aside. In a wok put the oil and when it smokes put the onions and garlic and fry well till golden brown. Add the ginger, turmeric, garam masala and salt to taste with half cup water. Add the tomatoes and sauté for a while. Put the spinach to boil with ¼ cup water on low heat till water comes out. Strain the spinach and put it in a blender, then mix the ground spinach with the meat and chopped coriander, Fry on high heat until all the water dries up. If frozen spinach is used defrost it first and press the water out. Sauté the mixture on medium heat till there is a little gravy. Turn off the heat.

Kabab (Mince Meat Kabab)

Ingredients

- 500 grams of minced goat meat
- ¼ cup chana dal (yellow lentils)
- 2 grated onions
- 3 heaped tsp ground garlic
- 1 chopped green chili
- 25 grams chopped coriander leaves
- 2 heaped tbsp ginger paste
- ½ tsp chili powder
- 3 tsp turmeric
- 3 tsp ground garam masala
- 1 egg (beaten)
- ¾ cup oil to fry + 1tbsp
- 4 tbsp of oil

Pressure-cook the minced meat for 2 minutes and dry out the water. Heat 1 tbsp of oil in a wok, fry the onion, garlic, until brown, then add all the other ingredients, and sauté for a bit except the egg. Cool the mixture and add the egg to the mince and blend till everything mixes. Take the mixture and make 6-8 portions. Flatten each portion into round flat shape. Take a frying pan, heat the oil and fry them 2 at a time on both sides. Place them on kitchen paper till the extra oil is soaked.

Murgi Methi (Chicken With Fenugreek Leaves)

Ingredients

- 1kg chicken legs and thighs
- 2 heaped tsp kasuri methi (dried methi powder)
- 2 cup chopped methi leaves
- 2 cup chopped coriander leaves
- 4 tsp turmeric powder
- 3 tsp garam masala powder
- 3 chopped onions
- 1 heaped tbsp of ginger paste
- 2 heaped tbsp garlic paste
- 2 tsp of sugar
- 3 tsp of lemon juice
- 4 tbsp mustard oil
- 1 tsp chili powder
- 2 cinnamon stick, 4 cardamom and 4 cloves
- Salt to taste

Heat the oil in a wok and fry the chicken legs and thighs very lightly and keep aside. In the same oil put the sugar, onions, and garlic, fry a little till it turns a golden color. Add the ginger, turmeric, garam masala powder and sauté for a bit with a sprinkling of water if required. Add salt, the fenugreek powder, lemon juice and 3 quarter cups of water. Pressure cook for 20 minutes, open the cooker and add the coriander leaves and fenugreek leaves till almost dry with very little gravy and ensure that the leaves are cooked well.

Murgi Sorse (Chicken With Mustard)

🥣 Ingredients

- 750 grams of chicken legs and thighs
- 1 cup beaten hung curd
- 2 tsp turmeric
- 1 tbsp ground fresh ginger
- ½ tsp chili powder or 2-3 green chili
- 5 tbsp mustard seeds, washed, ground and strained so that the coarse seed coats are removed
- 4 tbsp mustard oil
- Salt to taste

The mustard oil is about 3 tbsp to cook and another 1 tbsp. Put 3 tbsp of the oil on heat and sauté the chicken pieces till light brown in color. Add all the ingredients except the curd and mustard paste. Sauté for a bit add 3 quarter cups of water and pressure cook for about 20 minutes. Once the pieces are tender and the water has dried up, add the mustard seeds paste, the curd, quarter cup water and 1 tbsp of mustard oil. Mix and turn off heat.

Murgi Afgani (Chicken Afgani)

Ingredients

- 750 grams of boneless cubed chicken in small pieces
- 1 cup curd (hung to take the water out)
- 1 tbsp garlic
- 1 heaped tbsp ginger
- 1 ½ tsp ground garam masala
- Whole garam masala (3 cloves, 3 cardamom and 1 inch cinnamon stick)
- 1 tsp jaiphal
- 2 tsp sugar
- 10 soaked and ground almonds
- 1 tsp pepper corn roasted and ground
- 1 tbsp oil / ghee
- 4 tsp ground poppy seed
- Salt to taste

Marinate the chicken with curd, ginger, garlic, garam masala (ground), salt, sugar and jaiphal for 2 hrs. Heat the oil, add the whole garam masala and add the marinated chicken. Add ½ cup water and pressure cook for 20 minutes. When done put add the almonds, pepper corn and poppy seeds. Sauté till the gravy is thick. Turn off heat.

Metli Pyazkali (Goat Liver Curry With Spring Onion< Fenugreek And Corander Leaves)

Ingredients

- ½ kg goat liver cut in cubes
- 300 grams spring onions cut in 1inch pieces
- 1 cup chopped fenugreek leaves
- 1 cup chopped coriander leaves
- 1 heaped tbsp ginger paste
- 1 heaped tbsp garlic paste
- 1 tsp turmeric powder
- ½ tsp chili powder
- 2 tbsp mustard oil
- Salt to taste

In a wok heat the oil, when smoked lower the heat, put the garlic, turmeric, ginger and chili powder. Stir with a little water until the spices are well mixed. Add the spring onions, fenugreek and coriander leaves, turn up the heat to dry the water a little, add the liver and salt and cook till the water dries up.

Note: if you put the salt earlier, water will come out from the leaves and it will be difficult to dry out. Liver should not be cooked too long or else they become hard.

Green Chicken (Hariyali Chicken)

Ingredients

- 750 grams of boneless cubed chicken
- 3 tsp garlic
- 2 tsp ground ginger
- 2 tsp white pepper
- Crushed black sesame seeds (kalonji)
- 1 tsp clove powder
- 1 tsp cardamom powder (optional)
- 3 tbsp mustard oil
- ¾ cup of thick set hung curd (put on a strainer and drain water out)
- ½ cup mint leaves
- 1 cup coriander leaves/ paste
- 1 green chili
- Salt to taste

Marinate the chicken with all the above for 2 hrs, without the paste.

When ready to cook put the chicken cubes in a skewer, place the skewer on a shallow pan for the dripping. Broil under high heat for 15 minutes turning frequently to cook evenly.

The traditional method is to cook it on a charcoal grill. Haryali means green color, therefore the main ingredients in that kabab are green chilies, coriander leaves and mint leaves. When cooked put a little oil in a fry pan and sauté the chicken with a paste of coriander, mint and 1 green chilie.

Chutney

Aamsatyar Chutney (Dried Mango Chutney)

Ingredients

- 250 grams of aam satya (dried mango sheets sold as burfi)
- 75 grams of allu bokra (dried plum)
- ½ cup sugar
- 50 grams of black raisin
- 2 tsp white oil
- Juice of 1 lemon
- 1 tsp of panch phoron (whole 5 spices)
- ¼ tsp salt
- 2 tsp ground ginger
- 1 tsp turmeric powder

Cut the aam satya into 2 * 1inch pieces and put aside. Clean the allu bokra and soak for an hour, wash and soak the raisins. Smoke the oil and add the panch phoron and ginger, and turmeric. Put the aam satya into the oil, sauté with all the ingredients except sugar, mix well and add ½ or ¾ cup water. Boil aam satya and allu bokra in low heat till the water reduces, add the sugar and boil again till it becomes thick and sticky, add the lemon juice and take it off the fire.

Aamer Chutney (Raw Mango Chutney)

Ingredients

- 500 grams raw mangos peeled out and cut longitudinally with the seed taken out
- ¼ cup sugar or a little more
- 1 tsp of 5 spices (whole mixture of – coriander seeds, mustard seeds, cumin seeds, onion seeds, fenugreek seeds)
- Whole red chili (dried)
- 1 tsp turmeric
- 2 tsp mustard oil
- Salt to taste approx. ½ tsp

Heat the oil, the chili and 5 spices powder, when it sputters, add the cut mangoes, salt and turmeric, sauté and add 1 cup water. When the mangoes are a bit tender add sugar and boil till there is 1 cup gravy, Turn off the heat. It is normally eaten at the end of the main meal before dessert. It is supposed to clear the palate in preparation for the dessert.

Tomato Khejoor Chutney (Tomato And Date Chutney)

Ingredients

- 500 grams tomatoes (medium)
- 6 to 8 dates soaked for 1 hour
- ¼ cup raisin soaked for 1 hour
- 2 tsp panch phoron (whole spice)
- 1½ cup turmeric
- 1-2 dried red chili
- ½ cup sugar (a little more or less if the tomatoes are sour or sweet)
- ½ tsp salt

Cut the tomatoes in ¼ pieces deseed the dates and wash. Wash the raisins and take out the little stems. Heat the oil and when it smokes, lower heat add the tomatoes, dates and raisins, spices, turmeric, chilies and salt, sauté for a half minute. Pour ½ cup water cover and cook on lower heat until the tomatoes are soft. Then add the sugar and simmer further until the syrup is sticky but is of pouring consistency. Turn off the heat and serve hot or cold.

Breads
(Unleavened)

Luchi (Fried Bread)

Ingredients

- 1 ½ cup flour (white)
- 3 tsp oil or ghee
- 2 cups of white oil for frying
- Water for kneading the dough

Put the oil/ghee in the flour and mix well. Then add ½ cup water and mix the flour with it. Add more water to make a tight dough.

Make round balls from the dough about 20g to 25g each. Heat the oil in a wok on high heat, and when the oil smokes, reduce heat and roll out each ball into 3 inch diameter and fry one side then fry the other side till it is light brown, then take it off the oil and fry all of them the same way. If it is rolled out evenly the luchi will puff up into a round ball. It is served with any Indian dish.

Koraishuti Kocuri (Stuffed Fried Pea Bread)

🥣 Ingredients

- ½ kg peas ground to a paste with ¼ cup water and keep aside
- 2 cup white flour
- 4 tsp ghee + 2 tsp
- 2 heaped tsp ground ginger
- Chili powder to taste
- ½ tsp sugar
- ½ tsp cumin seeds (ground)
- 2 cups of white oil for frying
- Salt to taste

Sieve the flour and mix 4 tsp of ghee and when blended, add approx. ½ cup water and knead to a soft dough which is not very firm. Make little balls of 20 grams each and keep them covered so that they do not dry out.

Heat 2 tsp oil and when it smokes, lower the heat and add the ground peas and then add the ginger, chili powder, sugar, cumin seed powder and salt to taste, and sauté it till it dries.

The next step is a little difficult, but practice makes it simple. Make round balls about 15 grams approximately and stuff each of the pea balls into the dough balls, and roll out each of these in 3 inch diameter, making sure that the peas do not come out of the dough. It helps if you oil your fingers to make the pieces. Heat the oil and fry them like luchis, as above.

Radha Ballavi (Lentils Stuffed In Fried Bread)

🥣 Ingredients

- 2 cup flour (white)
- ½ cup water approx.
- ¾ cup urad dal
- 1 heaped tbsp fresh ground ginger
- ½ tsp chili
- 1 tsp whole kala jeera (kalonji)
- 1 tsp turmeric powder
- 1 tsp hing
- 4 cups or more oil to fry + 2 tbsp ghee
- Salt to taste

Soak the urad dal overnight and the next morning drain the water and grind to a paste with a little water. Mix the flour with the ghee and then add water to make a soft dough and keep aside. In a wok heat 1 tbsp oil. When it is hot add the urad dal paste, kalonji, ginger, turmeric, chili powder and hing. Sauté until the spices mix and the paste becomes soft and pliable. Then follow the same pattern as you would to make pea kochuri. Serve it with dum aloo or any other vegetable.

Cholar Daler Kochuri (Stuffed Fried Split Pea Bread)

 Ingredients

The same ingredients for pea kochuri except substitute peas with 1 cup cholar dal (chana dal)

Soak the lentils overnight in water and throw the water out before grinding it a fine paste with ¼ cup water.

Cook the stuffing in the same way as for pea kochuri that it is not too hard. Add the hing powder, mix it thoroughly and use it the same way as for pea kochuri.

Dalpuri (Unfried Split Pea Rolled Bread)

🥣 Ingredients

- 2 cups chana dal (split pea)
- 1 ½ cup flour
- ¼ cup water or more to knead the dough
- 4 tsp oil or ghee and ½ cup oil/ ghee for basting
- Chili powder to taste
- ½ tsp Sugar
- 1 heaped tsp ground ginger
- Salt to taste

Wash the dal and pressure cook it with 1½ cups of water so that the dal is cooked but keeps its shape and then grind it to a consistency to hold together into 15 gram balls. Add the dry spices, salt and mix well, and keep aside. Now add the 4 tsp oil/ ghee to the flour and knead the flour with water to a very soft dough. Take about 20 grams of the flour roll into a ball with the palm of your hand, then make a 20 grams ball of the dal stuffing and stuff it into each ball of dough to completely cover the stuffing. Seal the dough very well.

Roll each ball to about 5-inch diameter, adding a sprinkle of flour to make the rolling easier. They should be rolled out thin. Use a non stick fry pan and fry them one at a time on both sides. sprinkling 2 tsp oil*ghee or so for each piece. Take one out of the fry pan, put another 2 tsp of oil/ ghee and repeat till all are done. This really needs practice.

Bengali Desserts

STEAMED CHANAR PUDDING
(STEAMED COTTAGE CHEESE PUDDING)

🥣 Ingredients

- 400 grams of chana/paneer from any sweet shop
- 2 tbsp milk powder with ½ cup milk mixed in it
- 2 beaten eggs
- 2 tsp vanilla essence
- ½ cup sugar

Put the cottage cheese in the blender, add the thickened milk, and blend. Add the 2 eggs, sugar and vanilla essence and blend until everything is well mixed. Take a double boiler or in a pressure cooker add water and take a 8 inch cake tin. Pour the mixture in and place in the pressure cooker on a trivet and steam for 25-30 minutes but without the weight, you can also bake it in the oven of 180 for 25 minutes, but place the tin on a dish of water so that steam is produced. Take the tin out and chill it in the fridge for 2-4hrs. Cut in wedges and serve.

Payesh (Rice Pudding)

Ingredients

- 1 litre milk
- ¼ cup or little less small, grained basmati rice
- 4 tsp rose water
- ½ cup sugar
- 2 tbsp powdered milk

Grind the rice coarsely and set aside. Put the milk to boil after adding powdered milk. Boil for 3 minutes, then add the rice and lower heat until the milk thickens, the rice is done, then add the sugar. Boil for 2 minutes more, then add the rose water to the payesh. It should be thick but pouring consistency. Serve chilled. You can put a few rose petals on top.

Channnar Payesh (Cottage Cheese Pudding In Thickened Milk)

Ingredients

- 1 ltr of full-fat milk
- 250 grams channa (cottage cheese)
- 4-5 cardamoms
- 4 tsp rose water
- ¼ cup sugar
- 2 tbsp powdered milk

Channa is milk curdled into cheese (chana) and whey. You can do it at home by curdling milk with vinegar or lemon juice, but the easier option is to buy it in any sweet or vegetable shop/ supermarket.

Boil the milk, then lower the heat and let it thicken until it is about 1/3 the original quantity. Crush the cardamoms, milk powder, and sugar, boil it a little more till it is thick but pouring consistency. Grate the cheese and add it to the thickened milk. Mix well, add the rose water and chill it for an hour before serving.

Misti Doi (Sweet Youghurt)

Ingredients

- ½ liter milk (full fat)
- ½ tin condense milk
- 1 cup normal yoghurt beaten
- 1 tsp crushed cardamom seed
- 4 tsp sugar

Boil the milk slightly thickening it, add the condensed milk and cardamoms. Beat the yoghurt well and add it to the milk when it is a little warm like babies' bath water, Caramelize the sugar up to pouring consistency and add it the milk. Cover the mixture and keep it in a humid and warm place for 6 to 8 hours. When set, chill it in the fridge before serving.

Ice Cream Sandesh

Ingredients

- 300 grams chana (paneer/cottage cheese)
- 200 grams cream
- 4 tsp vanilla essence
- ½ cup caster sugar (powdered sugar)
- Pink coloring

Blend the chana in a blender until it is smooth, and add sugar and the cream, vanilla, and blend until the mixture is very smooth and well mixed. Use a drop of pink coloring during blending. Pour it in a shallow container about 1 ½ inch in height.

Smoothen it, cover with cling film and freeze for 5 hours approx. Take it out 15 minutes before serving. Cut in squares and serve. You can garnish with rose petals if you wish.

Kheer Sandesh

Ingredients

- 100 grams of khoa (thickened milk which comes in a block at any sweet shop)
- 500 grams of chana (cottage cheese)
- 200 ml of condensed milk
- ¼ tsp saffron

Soak the saffron in ¼ cup milk. Blend the paneer till creamy, add the khoa, blend till smooth, add the condensed milk and again blend till everything is mixed properly.

In a wok under low heat sauté the mixture until it dries up, and becomes a soft but solid mass add the saffron, and spread it on a nonstick plate, and smooth the top, cool it, and place it in the fridge for 2-3 hrs. take a sharp knife and cut it into 2*2 squares and serve.

If you wish, put a drop of orange coloring to the saffron milk to give the Sandesh some color.

Narkol Naru

Ingredients

- 1 freshly grated coconut freshly
- 50g of khoa (thickened milk in blocks available in sweet shop)
- 1/2 of gur (jaggery) or if not available use ½ cup sugar

Grate the khoya finely and set aside. The jaggery should be good quality and is made from sugarcane or date tree and has a very flowery scent.

Heat the wok, and add the sugar/jaggery, coconut and stir under medium heat till the water dries up. Put the khoa and sauté till the consistency is sticky which is then made into 20 gram round balls while it Is hot. It will be harden a bit when cooled down.

Rosogullar Payesh (Cottage Cheese Balls In Thickened Milk)

🥣 Ingredients

- 8 to 10 rasogullas medium size from any sweet shop
- 750ml of full cream milk
- ½ cup sugar
- 2 tbsp heaped powdered milk
- 10 to 12 sliced pistachios

Squeeze the rosogolla and take out the syrup and keep aside. Mix the milk, sugar and powdered milk and boil till it is to half quantity reduced. Put the rosogollas into it and turn the heat off. Add the pistachios. Refrigerate for 2 hrs before serving.

Chanar Malpua (Fried Cottage Cheese In Syrup)

🥣 Ingredients

- ½ cups cottage cheese
- 2 tablespoons dried milk powder
- ¾ cup milk
- ½ tsp salt
- 1½ tsp corn flour
- 1 tsp cardamom seeds
- 1 cup sugar
- 2 tsp ghee + ½ cup oil to shallow fry

Blend the cottage cheese and powdered milk into a fine paste. Add milk with the corn flour, ghee, and salt and blend with the cheese to make a thick batter. Add the cardamom seeds to it. Take a non-stick fry pan and put some ghee to smear the pan. With 1 cup sugar and water make a medium consistency syrup which is sticky.

Smoke a little oil in the fry pan, lower heat and pour the cheese mixture with a ladle and spread the mixture evenly to make a 3-inch round shape, pour a tsp of oil all around the edge of the batter, then flip it to cook on the other side. Once both sides are golden brown, drop the malpua into the syrup. You make 4 at a time in the frying pan if it has a larger base. There should be 10-12 pieces. Leave them in the syrup for 2-3 hours till the malpuas soak up the syrup. If you find that there should be more syrup, prepare it and pour it over all the pieces to soak.

Notes

Other Recipes

Cheeesecake

This cheesecake has minimum calories as it is not made with cream cheese but is made with curdled milk.

🥣 Ingredients

1 ½ litre of whole boiling milk. In ½ cup water add 1 tbsp lemon juice or 2 tsp white vinegar. As the milk boils, lower the heat to minimum and start pouring the sour water, keep stirring till you find that the milk separates into curd and whey. Once the curd is well formed, it will separate from the whey. Leave it in a colander to drain excess water.

- 2 cups of yoghurt and strain it to get rid of excess water
- 2 beaten eggs
- 6 to 8 large, digestive biscuits made into fine bread crumbs
- 100 ml of cream
- 3 quarter cup caster sugar
- 2 tsp corn flour
- 4 tsp vanilla essence
- 4 tsp of butter
- ½ lemon zest
- ½ cup lemon juice
- Pinch of salt

Mix the biscuit crumbs with 4 tsp butter, line a 10-inch pie dish, line it with crumbs and press it down evenly and microwave it for about ½ minute take it out and cool.

In the meantime, take a large bowl, mix the beaten eggs with 3 quarter cup caster sugar, 2 tsp corn flour, 2 tsp vanilla essence and the salt. Put the hung curd in a blender and blend it. Add it to the egg mixture put ½ cup lemon juice and the cream, blend well, and when the mixture is smooth pour it on the crumble base and sprinkle with 1 tsp full zest of half a lemon. Place it in a pre-heated oven for 25 minutes at 180 degrees and take it out and leave it in the fridge to set.

Note: Instead of making the cottage cheese at home you can buy 300 grams of cottage cheese to use in the cheesecake

Chocolate Cake

Everyone seems to be partial to chocolates, and there is a way of making simple homemade chocolate cakes to have any time, tea, coffee or even as a dessert, served with a dollop of fresh cream or chocolate sauce.

Ingredients

- 1 ½ cups flour
- 1 tsp baking soda
- 1 ½ tsp baking powder
- ¾ cup 85% cocoa or unsweetened chocolate powder
- 1 ½ cup sugar
- ½ cup oil
- ¼ cup butter
- 3 eggs
- 1 cup milk
- ½ cup hot water
- 2 tsp vanilla essence
- 1 tsp salt

Pre heat the oven at 180 degrees Celsius. Mix all the dry ingredients and pass through a sieve and keep. With a beater, beat the eggs well. Add the oil and butter and beat, add the sugar, and beat until light and fluffy. Add the vanilla and milk and then add the dry mixture gradually. Grease a 10*10-inch pan or a 6*12-inch pan or even a round 8inch pan and dust it with flour. Add the hot water to the mixture and beat everything clockwise. Do not overheat. The batter should be neither thick nor thin, add the water accordingly. It should be of thick pouring consistency.

Pour it in the pan and even out the batter by lightly shaking the pan so that there is no air. Place it in the oven and bake for 40 minutes. Stick a toothpick in the center to test if it is cooked through. Gently take it out of the pan and turn it over to cool on a rack. If you wish drizzle shop bought chocolate sauce over it.

Apple Layer Cake

Ingredients

- Peel and grate 3 small or 2 large apples and squeeze 1 tsp lemon juice to prevent from coloring
- Mix with 3 tsp cinnamon and 2 tsp nut meg powder and keep aside
- In a bowl add
- 1 cup flour
- 1 ½ tsp baking powder
- 1 cup sugar
- ½ cup semolina
- 1 cup milk
- ¼ cup oil

Take a cup of milk and add ¼ cup oil and mix well. Line a 8-inch pan with 1/3 of the apples and cover evenly with ¼ of the dry ingredients in layers till all the apples are used.

Set the oven at 180 degrees, for 35 minutes. Prick the contents of the pan with a fork and pour the milk and oil mixture on it evenly. Place it in the oven. The cake when cut will come out in layers.

Plain Vanilla Cake (Eggless)

🥣 Ingredients

- 1 2/3 cup flour
- 1 cup caster sugar
- 1 tsp baking soda
- ½ tsp baking powder
- ½ tsp salt
- 3 tsp vanilla essence
- ½ cup oil /butter (melted)
- ½ cup yoghurt and ½ cup water (whisked together)
- An 8' round cake pan oil and dusted with flour

Heat oven at 180 degrees Celsius. Mix the dry ingredients together and keep aside. Beat the oil/butter with the vanilla, yogurt and add the dry mixture. Mix everything together and bake for 35 minutes. Skewer the center of the cake to check that it comes out clean and dry. Tip it out of the pan and let it cool. Serve it with vanilla sauce chocolate sauce or use it as a base for a fruit gateau. It is a simple cake for vegetarians.

Notes

Help Notes

Below are some help notes which might be of use while cooking these recipes.

In Bengal rice is normally strained after cooking by pouring boiling water over it in a strainer so that the grains separate well and also remove the excess starch to lower the calories.

Some vegetables such as aubergines, absorb a lot of oil while frying so spray oil on them and grill under medium heat (till golden brown), though frying delivers a better taste.

Try to put tomatoes last in cooking as the sourness prevents other vegetables from cooking through. This applies to yogurt and vinegar as well.

When cooking in a pressure cooker, the water should be as much as you want to make the gravy. If it is too much, it will be watery (unless you want to throw out the water after cooking).

Most dishes are cooked in mustard oil, which has a pungent smell and is an acquired taste. Other oils may be use and will result in a different flavor.

Garlic and onions are not always used in vegetarian dishes unlike other Indian states.

Generic names indicate the style of preparation of dishes:

- Dalna – Vegetarian curry with gravy.

- Kalia – A non-vegetarian curry with onions and garlic (typically fish curry).

- Bati Charchari – A dish which is prepared by putting all the spices, salt, oil etc., and steamed / baked (easier in a microwave).

- Ghonto – A dry vegetable curry with many vegetables in it and grated coconut. A non-vegetarian version has onions, fish but no coconut.

- ❯ Charchari – A dry mixed vegetable curry which has any mixture of vegetables in it.

Bengali deserts are all milk based, and sweet shops are seen in almost every street corner. Most are bought at shops but the recipes here are fairly simple.

Weights and measures:

In the past, we used a common teaspoon for measuring everything and some of it was hit or miss. We can use measuring spoons today so we can be more accurate. All recipes in this book are in standard measures.

The number of people eating a dish is not indicated because in this style of cuisine, two, four or even six different items are served during the meal. However, for a general measure, each recipe serves approximately 4-5 people.

The Indian teacup measures 150 grams, but the American cup measure 250 grams. These recipes use standard Indian cup measure.

NAME OF INGREDIENTS (BENGALI TO ENGLISH)

BENGALI	ENGLIGH
CHAL	RAW RICE
BHAT	COOKED RICE
DAL	LENTIL
SHAK	LEAFY VEGETABLE (EX-SPINACH)
DHANE PATTA	CORIANDER
PUDINA	MINT
METHI	FENUGREEK
SHARSHE SHAK	MUSTARD
LAU	BOTTLE GOURD
KUMRA	PUMPKIN
BEGUN	AUBERGINE/BRINJAL
ALLOO	POTATO
PYAZZ SAK	ONION PLANT
RASUN	GARLIC
SHARSE	MUSTARD SEEDS
POSTO	OPIUM SEEDS
KALO JEERA	ONION SEEDS
HING	ASAFOETIDA
PANCH PHORON	5 SPICES (WHOLE MIXED – ONION SEED, CORIANDER SEED, MUSTARD SEED, CUMIN SEED, FENUGREEK SEED)
TEJ PATTA	BAY LEAF
KANCHA LANKA	GREEN CHILI
SHUKNO LANKA	DRY CHILI
PHOOL KOPI	CAULIFLOWER
BANDHA KOPI	CABBAGE
KARAISHUTI	PEAS
TOMATO	TOMATO
LEBOO	LIME
CHEENI	SUGAR

Contd…

BENGALI	ENGLIGH
NOON	SALT
GUR	JAGGERY
KACHA AAM	RAW MANGO
BEAN	FRENCH BEAN
CHICHINGA	SNAKE GOURD
AMCHUR	POWDERED DRIED RAW MANGOES
AAM	RIPE MANGO
KHEJUR	DATES
KISMISH	RAISINS
AAMSATTA	SUNDRIED MANGO JUICE MADE INTO BLOCKS
CHANNA	COTTAGE CHEESE
KHOYA	THICKENED MILK (DRIED)
GAJJAR	CARROT
BEET	BEETROOT
SHOSHA	CUCUMBER
MAIDA	FLOUR (REFINED)
ATTA	WHEAT FLOUR
SARSE TEL	MUSTARD OIL
SADATEL	WHITE OIL
GHEE	CLARIFIED BUTTER
DALCHINI	CINNAMON
CHOTO ELACHI	CARDOMOM
LABANGA	CLOVE
MAURI	FENNEL
DUDH	MILK
GARAM MASALA	MIXED ALL SPICE (CARDAMOM, CINNAMON, JEERA, CORRIANDER, METHI, CUMIN, GINGER CLOVES GROUND TOGETHER)
DHANE	CORIANDER SEEDS
JEERA	CUMIN
HALUD	TURMERIC

BENGALI	ENGLIGH
ADA	GINGER
UCCHE	BITTER GOURD
CHICHINGA	SNAKE GOURD
AENCHOR	RAW JACKFRUIT
NARKOL	COCONUT
BHINDI	OKHRA/LADIES FINGER
GOL MORICH	BLACK PEPPER
JAIPHAL	NUTMEG
DOI	YOGHURT
ALOO BUKRA	DRIED PLUMS
MALAI	CREAM
POTOL	PALWAL (NO OTHER ENGLISH NAME)
JAITRI	JAVITRI
JAFFRAN	SAFRON
MOORO	FISH HEAD
METLI	LIVER
GULAB JOL	ROSE WATER
SUJI	SEMOLINA

Beguner Raita (Bringal withYougurt) — Posto
(Opium Seeds, Khuskhus)

Beet Chop (Beetroot Croquete) — Lau Chingri
(Gourd with Shrimp)

Chingri malai curry(Prawn with coconut milk) — Palang Sak (Fried spinach) — Bhat(Rice)

Luchi (Fried bread) — CholarDal (Split Pea)

Misti Bhat. (Sweet Rice) — Dahi Mach
(Fish with Youghurt)

Murgi Afghani (Chicken Afgani) — Dahi Mach
(Fish with Yoghurt)

Tomato KhejurChutney
(Tomato and Date Chutney) — Arhaar Dal

Koraisutir Kochori (Fried Pea stuffed bread) — Chanar and payesh (Cottage Cheese in thickened milk)

NarkalNaru (Grated coconut balls in sugar) — Kheer Sandesh (Thickened milk with Cottage Cheese)

Sukto (Mixed veg curry with bitter gourd) — Mocha
(Banana Flower)